Reflections of the Heart

Bridget Robinson

Reflections of the Heart

Bridget Robinson

REFLECTIONS OF THE HEART

By Bridget Robinson

Cover Photography by: Houston Deberry Photography
Cover design by: Denilson Sibrian

Scripture quotations are from The Holy Bible, Old and New Testaments, by Holman Bible Publishers Nashville, Copyright 1979

ISBN: 9781653868544

ACKNOWLEDGMENT

This book is dedicated to my children Tay Roper, Nyle Roper, Nya Roper, and god-daughter Raychele Walls, my true inspirations in life. God has blessed me with words that I hope will touch each of you the way they have inspired me to write these pieces. Someone once asked me if I was a writer. I said, oh no, not me, I just dibble and dabble in it. They told me to own it and believe in myself and just do it, thanks Mr. James Brooks. So now, when you ask me if I am a writer? I respond, Yes, I write inspirational poetry!

Also, I would like to thank my friends and family that challenged, counseled, inspired, coached, encouraged, loved me and insisted I publish and share these writings with the world. Just to name a few of you:

- My father, the belated James Earl Robinson, we had so many talks about Proverbs 4:23 *Keep thy HEART with all diligence: for out of it are the ISSUES of life*. Thank you for listening and understanding me. Your guidance played an integral part in helping me to become the purpose filled person I am today. I miss you here on earth, but all of the memories we shared will never be forgotten.

- My mother, Stella L. Robinson, the strongest, most vibrant, talented and gifted woman of God I know. Mom, I truly appreciate every hug, every encouraging word, me seeing you on your knees praying and reading the word, your support and love you have shown me and my children. Thank you.

- My aunt, Vicki Robinson, you read my piece of work and immediately said this has to be shared with the world. Thank you for that first initial push, that made me believe—that yes, I should publish my poems. Because of that spoken word, this inspirational poetry book is now a reality. And one day soon will be performed at Spoken Word and Poetry Readings across the world.

- My siblings: Vanesia Wright, Jamie Robinson, and Tawanna Sargent, thank you sisters, your baby sister loves you so very much for always being there encouraging, challenging, and loving me no matter what. Love you sweet, creative, gifted, powerful women of God. .

iv

CONTENTS

PREFACE

The pieces in this book come from times of growth, joy, peace, sacrifice, and brokenness throughout life. Life has a way of bringing out the best in us, the good and the bad. The main poem, Tree Connection will leave you asking yourself, Will you sway? Will you stay rooted? Who's tying you down? Who's poking you? Will life cause you to be crooked? Will you flourish? Will you die? Will you lean? Will you bend? Is there truly a connection between trees and a person?

Some will doubt the connection of a tree to a live person, but this poem will answer their doubt. It will challenge you to look at where your strength comes from in relation to that of an actual tree planted here on earth. Reflect on your life story of testing who you really are when life challenges you with raining cats and dogs, clear skies ahead, to sleeting and hailing all over.

As you continue to inhale and exhale while reading this poem, the next few poems will have your heart racing and excited to read more. If you have ever lost a loved one, a friendship, a relationship, or even a job, you will and can relate to the poems in this book. These inspiring poems will take you on intimate thrills in and around relationships.

A path of emotions—through love, turmoil, struggle, identity loss, and society trying to define you. But through it all, the poems will touch your heart and leave you with real life encounters of encouraging uplifting words. Don't stop now, read and enjoy the ride.

TREE CONNECTION

A *strong storm* passes through and causes the tree to be uprooted. Some trees will die inside. And some will die outside.

Sometimes a strong and firm tree will stay rooted and continue to thrive and hold their endurance after the storm passes.

Where are you Rooted?

After a storm you have some trees that are re-planted, re-birthed and they re-establish their roots and grow stronger over time.

Some newly planted trees will establish new roots on solid ground, some on rocky ground and some will simply be tied down.

Imagine two newly planted trees side by side in the same soil, and same foundation. As you watch the trees grow, one tree will establish a strong foundation in their roots. Another tree could possibly lack a strong foundation and its roots *will not* stay rooted.

One will grow leaves. The leaves might even go through *seasonal changes and flourish* and become pleasing to the eye.

Its beauty is gorgeous, colorful, peaceful, and a delight to watch.

Its vibrant sway of its leaves will waver back and forth given the appearance it can't be touched.

But when it is *STILL*, that is when only the *RIGHT touch* will appear. This tree could touch ones heart in unimaginable ways.

Let us not forget the other tree that was planted at the same time. This tree will not grow leaves. It will give the impression that something has happened to it. This tree shows no life. Or does it? It appears that nothing is there. It is incomplete! It is not as pleasing to the eye.

Some would say it is just there taking up space as that of a tree **stump**. BUT wait, it is not completely dead.

Remember, appearances are deceiving and can change in *an instance. Some trees will ignite without notice.*

Due to an igniting occurrence this tree might grow one leaf. It will hold on for dear life, while the other tree will have several leaves and it will hold on to something bigger than life. *Or are both trees holding onto something bigger than life?*

Season Changes

Trees go through many seasonal changes. Some grow really tall, and some average height and some are just short. Some are fat, some are average size, some are skinny, and some do not grow at all.

Their vigorous existence here on earth will cause them to change their colors. And YES, their true colors will start to shine through while they conform to life's many changes.

Due to seasonal changes and time, some will start to lean and curve.

Some curve into many directions, thus branching out, curving over, curving downward, and sometimes upward. Some might even change directions with the wind or the storms passing through. Some might even start to separate and branch out away from what is holding it together and eventually fall off. Some trees will become crooked.

Some will become frail, or brittle. Some could possibly **poke** you or *cut* you. Some will develop diseases. Some will heal you. Some will have a scent about them. Some develop and aura and some an odor.

Some trees know how to shake things off of them; and some simply hold onto everything.

Some trees will demand attention. Some trees are protected by others and some trees do the protecting. The protectors will stand guard, tall and firm.

There are trees used for other things. Some trees are walked on. Some trees are carved on.

Some trees come with attachments. Some trees provide fruits. Some trees devour fruits. Some trees are rotten. Some trees can **snap** without notice.

Some trees will stand alone and will have the appearance of being cold and/or lonely. Some trees will stand together allowing others to lean on them as a result holding them up. Some trees will gravitate towards others. Some trees will attract others. Some trees are intertwined and truly divine while others do not partake of THE vine.

Some trees allow light to shine on them to receive nourishment and thirst for nothing. Consequently, allowing others to use them to supply food for others to eat.

However. rebellious trees will reject proper nourishment, not allowing others to use them and they tend to bare no fruits. Some might consider these to be hollow or even rotten trees. Thus all dried up. Even though it absorbs anything and everything it comes in contact with.

Some trees get labeled. Some are considered amazing, charming and they manifest into something beautiful. Some are considered odd, rough, and unattractive. These trees are *sometimes* hindered and never reach their full potential.

All trees have a *perfect* uniqueness about them.

A tree is life, it has character, and it gives words. What has the storm done to your tree?

Written By: Bridget Robinson -- November 24, 2011

Proverbs 13:12   Unrelenting disappointment leaves you heart sick, but a sudden good break can turn life around (A TREE of LIFE)

Dedicated to and inspired by my late father
James Earl Robinson

INSECURITIES

Why do you look at me -- Stop looking at me -- Don't
you see -- I'm insecure in my own *Insecurities* --
Wrapped up in rejection -- that has become my
reflection -- oh what a slap to any reputation -- I'm
shut up and all wrapped up in this thing called
Insecurity

It's all around me -- can't seem to break free -- From
every uncertainty and negativity -- That pool of
insanity -- that is the existence of its vanity -- Causing
Unswerving, undetaining, unimaginable, uncontrolling
paining -- It has transformed me and criticized me and
deserted me

Don't look -- Don't look -- it won't stop

It's captured me -- It's taken hold of me -- Its anxiety,
is that of deity -- Its priority, is that of desire in me –

How will I stand, How will I fight, Its hold -- is just
too tight -- The pressure, The pressure, of Society
looking at me -- Oh who will I be, Do I have it in me,
the need to feel sure of me -- That insecurity, yep it
Reigned all over me -- Oh where oh where could I be –

Why am I filled with such *unsurety* -- Could this be a
game, oh don't you see -- Every inch of me -- fighting
this insecurity -- This was not a game but you didn't
feel the same – for you had the ability to make a
change -- when they called out your name – for you
could have claimed that assumed name. -- It's just an
observation but who caused this transformation –

This dejection, this causation that is disabling me, paining me, and causing this uncertainty -- Oh was it me?

But wait, -- NOW Look -- No Stop, -- AND Look -- For my body shook -- That insecurity -- it was just a crook -- That took -- what I thought was the unsure me -- That was just the world's reality -- Which has no relativity -- And is not my assurity into my security -- the true me -- what my existence is you see -- is what HE thinks of me -- HE has rescued me -- and turned my insecurities into my security -- You ask are you sure it's HE -- That's Filled you with this sense of security -- I respond and say, Joy Is in HE and He grants my security -- No more *unsurety*, no more *uncertainty*, no more *insecurities*.

Those *insecurities* that brought me to my knees – that nearly defined me -- But did not design me -- For HE saw the true me and personified the deity in me -- For now I see -- HE has truly turned my *insecurities* into my Security and truly inspired me to be someone with proclaiming security.

Written By: Bridget Robinson

THE 1

No more running!
No more wanting to escape!
When you finally meet **THE 1!**
Everything you once hoped for
Appeared through the door
His whisper captured my heart
THE 1 you want to spend every
moment with!
THE 1 to hear his voice,
places fear at a loss!

You ask, fear of what?
Fear of love, Fear of pain, Fear of rejection,
Fear of knowing his name,
I know -- that is lame
When you find **THE 1**
Each thought of you makes my heart melt
THE 1 that I will begin my day with
THE 1 that I will end my day with
THE 1 that I admire and ignites a fire
The 1 that truly inspires!

Written By: Bridget Robinson

BE STILL IN LOVE

The words drifted from my Soul
Like a Beam of Gold
The silliness of Laughter
Beams like a Ray of Light
The joy of his Rapture
Cultivates in Capture
Each smile sends spasms
To the jaw line
To a once Profound Frown
The LORD works through me
In me
And with me
As Gravity
Tries to Devour me
IT STOPS!
It was once Fear
That was so Dear to me
That Brought Turmoil
Self Gratification and
Self Doubt
But Flees with its Mound
As COURAGE Flourishes
And indeed Surmounts

Written By: Bridget Robinson

Poem Dedication: To the one trapped into destiny and not turning back!

BEAUTIFUL

I'm beautiful,

I love all of me,

every curve,

every pimple,

every imperfection

that makes it perfection.

I love all of me!

Written By: Bridget Robinson

FOR ME

God I found you!

I remember when I use to speak to you

And you would speak to me

When silence happened

The devil said you were mad at me

But I knew that was not meant for me

I can never measure the love you have for me

The kind that pours out for me

Endless Love that truly protects me

Your Love -- it is for me.

Written By: Bridget Robinson

MISTAKES

I held your hand, I led the way

I tried to teach You, the right way

You pushed my buttons

We disagreed

You felt grown, and decided to leave

You shouted in frustration

Your voice sent vibrations

Your words like daggers

Rapidly flying without stagger

Your temper boileth

You were angry

You were hurting

You were borderline un-taming

You couldn't see

what tempted thee

And caused You to make

Your biggest mistake

Didn't You wonder

What was at stake

As it wasn't meant

To cause this big mistake

Wouldn't it be nice if one could only

retake

what feels

is that big mistake

You were unhappy

Over took by pride

At that place

You were a disgrace

But thank GOD

you are still alive

Because that mistake

That had You to believe

You were able to do

Whatever You please

It fueled the fire

But Must Expire

Because of GOD's grace

You were able to retake

What one feels

Are those big mistakes

For those mistakes

Were not made

To be rubbed

In ones face

When You love

When You truly love

Like the Father loves

Those daggers that fly

Off your tongue

With Intentions of

Doing so much Harm

Those words

Will not stay

For they will not stay

In a space

That has no place

Beside GOD's GRACE

Those words

Oh but those words

Will now fall

On their face

As I intend to replace it

With those words

That you did not say

For it was by GOD's Grace

That caused me to stay

In this place,

That I embrace

I welcome you home

With open arms

As You proceed

To retake

those learned Mistakes

For I will not continue

To retrace your mistakes

And cause You harm or disgrace

For my love for You

Will always replace

All of your

learned mistakes

Now go Bake in it

And put your best in it

And let GOD's Grace

Embrace and Shine in it

Written By: Bridget Robinson

IN YOUR GRIPS

As I slip away

You want me to stay

You paved the way

But I want it my way

When You hold me by day

I pull away and stray

But, You are still, never so far away

Although unknowingly, I try and keep you at bay

Your touch of comfort, asks me to stay

You have your way of reaching all of me

And all of me, only You can see

With no delay

I allow myself to let go and pray

A hold of me today

In your grips, I will stay

Please continue to come **my way**

As I squeeze you day to day

My way, becomes your way

And your way, is where I want to stay.

Written By: Bridget Robinson

WHY ARE YOU IN MY LIFE?

Why are you in My Life?

Did you come that I shall grow

Did you come that I shall sow

Did you come that I shall know

Oh why oh why are you in my Life

Why are you in My Life?

Did you come to invest in me

Did you come to bring out the best in me

Did you come to test me

Oh why oh why are you in my Life

Why are you in My Life?

Did you come to learn from me

Did you come to rain on me

Did you come out of concern for me

Oh why oh why are you in my Life

Why are you in My Life?

Did you come to bless me

Did you come to pull out the worst in me

Did you come to pour into me

Oh why oh why are you in my Life

Why are you in My Life?

Did you come to walk out the door

Did you come to see me roar

Did you come to see me soar

Oh why oh why are you in my Life

Why are you in My Life?

Did you come to be my captain

Did you come to help me over the mountain

Did you come to be my fountain

Oh why oh why are you in my Life

Why are you in My Life?

Did you come to take over me

Did you come to speak over me

Did you come to be a part of me

Oh why oh why are you in my Life

Why are you in My Life?

You came

To be one with me

To navigate me

To restore me

To complete me

To love me

To pour into me

To grow me

To never leave me

To never forsake me

Thank you for being the *ONE* for me

Written By: Bridget Robinson

THAT

THAT you would be
All THAT you could be
So THAT you could mean
THAT much more to me

THAT you would know
In all THAT you show
In all THAT you sow
How much THAT you grow

I appreciate THAT growth in thee
And THAT presence we all see
Let THAT light continue to shine in thee

Like THAT of a Firelight
Continue THAT Fight
Despite THAT Night
For in THAT Strife
Shine THAT Bright
As THAT of a night Firelight

Written By: Bridget Robinson

Dedicated to Mary Davis a challenge of 'THAT'

BRIDGET ROBINSON

TO GIVE UP ON LOVE -- IS TO GIVE UP ON YOU

To experience excitement
To experience emotion
To experience passion
To experience power
To experience exuberance
Just -- to experience LOVE

To experience connection
To experience reflection
To experience fascination
To experience affection
To experience admiration
Just -- to experience LOVE

To experience fondness
To experience sweetness
To experience togetherness
To experience tenderness
To experience Captiveness
Just -- to experience LOVE

To experience Fearlessness
To experience Dearness
To experience Appreciativeness
To experience Angelicness
To experience Oneness
Just -- to experience LOVE

To experience sharing
To experience daring
To experience swearing
To experience bearing
To experience caring
Just -- to experience LOVE

To experience serving
To experience giving
To experience holding
To experience adoring
To experience cherishing
Just -- to experience LOVE

To experience a smile
To experience for a while
To experience what the heart--truly desires
JUST -- TO -- EXPERIENCE -- LOVE

Written By: Bridget Robinson

CHAIN REACTION

I was at the end of my rope hopeless

filled with pain from whom I thought you were.

I was Godless, Powerless, and Rageless.

You blindsided me with your craftiness.

Your schemes were skillful.

For my brain you dissected like a fetal pig tearing

up my insides examining every part of me

Identifying my weaknesses,

Identifying your insecurities that you

forced on me,

Identifying every apology that I gave to you

because of your twisted ways and guilty emotions.

Yet you still self-perpetuated dwelling on your

negative days and ways.

For your betrayal ----- imbalanced me,

Your trickery ----- nearly destroyed me.

You exploited my organs putting me on display.

Breaking my heart in unimaginable ways.

I sacrificed, I loved, I understood, I had a
compassion, but you took an action
screechhhhhhhhhhhhhhhhhhhhhhhhh.
Chain reaction
For you were intoxicating and obliterating
For I didn't know you laid me out like bait
For your words sent me into a comatose state

OH you can't relate, oh let me translate
You're in pain, you can't focus on your own
inadequacies,
So you project your self-perpetuating acts on
others
Your deflection manifestation is on point
you assume you are superior
when indeed you become inferior
your Freudian Projection -- denying existence of
oneself –
Cause you to say it's not me it's you.
[Dysfunction junction that is your function]

For your fears I'm not trying to steal

For your guilt Wrap it up in a quilt

For your denial It's not in my profile

For my revolving door is no more

For you tried to make me your New Year's

resolution,

But my God, made you part of the solution

For it was my fate that God chose to resuscitate

Causing my heart rate to beat at a natural state.

If there is ever a possibility you will make a

mistake

to attack my very own heart rate.

I declare right now with every trace of his blood

that runs within me,

I am secure, yes, I said secure

IN GOD's hands.

Written by: Bridget Robinson

ESCAPE

The rocks pelted my body
Pushing me back with every shot,
breakup after breakup,
hurt after hurt,
Heartbreak after heartbreak,
failure, defeat, pressure, the rape,
physical and emotional abuse

I'm surrounded by sorrow,
Buried by an Avalache
Genesis 19:17 "… Escape for Your Life"

I FIGHT
To Escape the Corruption
I FIGHT
To Escape the Destruction
I FIGHT
To Escape the Disruption
Butttttt the trap
slapped a strait jacket on me

with every past fault,
IT TIGHTENS

Depression, Anxiety, Addictions
IT TIGHTENS

Upsets, Doubt, Division
IT TIGHTENS

Lack of motivation, sin, divorce,
IT TIGHTENS

And did I mention the disappointment that
Torched my skin like a thermal incinerator

A quiet whisper amplifies the air . . .
E-s-c-a-p-e for y-o-u-r L-i-f-e-e-e-e-e

I FIGHT!
The Challenges fly at me
at the speed of the world's fastest bullet train

I Lose Focus!
The tramplings of fear try and overtake me

I'm Frantic!
I scream: I'm Broken,
I step forward, I step back
I hear
Escape For Your Life

Tears of pain rush in like a flood
With no Noah's Arc in sight.

Attack, Survive,
ESCAPE FOR YOUR LIFE

I fall to my knees, Lord Jesus Please
My trust is in you!
and
For he was pleased

I escaped like a bird from the hunters' trap
My help, oh yes, it was in the name of thy most
high!
Victory in its most exhilarating form
Radiating from my body

A profound glow of growth
Encapsulated my words,
my thoughts, my actions

oh Thank You Lord,

For I was not consumed
Nor did I LOOK behind me
Thank you Father for saving me
For renewing me
For helping me
I ESCAPED
WITH *MY* LIFE!

Written by: Bridget Robinson

WITHIN

*I'm just a person chasing dreams while
fears chase me*

*Fears of being alone— fears of hope not
finding its way home*

*Fears of defeat over articulating what
I'm meant to be*

*Some see the me that stands before
thee, and*

some see the me that I can be

*But what they see in me doesn't matter
to me,*

when I allow my fears to annihilate me.

*That feeling of defeat captures me at
my feet,*

*causing me to retire that fire that could
inspire my*

*every bone to rejuvenate my every
harvest.*

They say I see so much potential in you.

They say I see you have a calling over your life.

They say I see A light in you.

But me, through fear, what I see, is a less potential state.

Through fear, I see a calling to call for help.

Through fear, I see a light that's not meant for me,

maybe it's meant for you—you see.

But without fear, I see, what I would like to be

with My Ambitions you see

being upmost capable to do exceedingly above and beyond.

*But... that call from within, allows the
fears to annihilate me.*

*Why can't I expire that fear and let the
empowering of fear reveal its true colors
to me*

*Can't fear see, from within,
I inspire to be someone as great as he.*

To stop people in their tracks.

To be more powerful than thoughts.

*To be the type of relationship everyone
interacts with.*

*To positively stretch me past my
comfort zone.*

*To be more calculating and decisive
beating the odds creating an
atmosphere that withstands pressures.*

*To instill growth and commitment as a
constant reminder I'm still there.*

*To make you pass and think and run
and retreat, but that's just hesitation
from within and is not meant for you to*

depend on it and run and retreat as you pass up

every opportunity because

Fear is wrestling with your purpose and strongest part of your intelligence

in what transpires to be

the life that's meant for thee not he.

But truly from within, doesn't fear feel like a sin?

Prowling around seeking to devour with every chance you let your emotions

overtake your every thought, Controlling you, and making you ever more anxious.

Consuming you, abusing you, shaming you, unrightfully wronging you.

I finally stop and write to you Fear,

From within—Fear, we are friends. We started out with a love hate relationship. But through time, I learned when you paralyzed me, from within—I internalized thee and allowed my emotions to get the best of me. But this time fear, I dealt with you directly you see. You are not meant to annihilate me, you are meant to fuel me and protect me. I recognize you and embrace the success you have brewed in me. You PREPARED FOR ME, You SOAKED ME! BOILED ME! PRESSED ME! PICKED ME! You Came At Me!

Oh my beloved fear! You No Longer Control Me! I embrace

thee! And Grow from thee! I'm now Free to be that strong type of fear that is within me.

That relentless one, the aware one, the one that's equipped and powerful, the one that stands strong. My within has endless ends.

Written by: Bridget Robinson

Special Tribute from my Daughter Nya Roper

WORDS

I'm clueless
These dark blue seas
I am tired of them putting me down
But they will not get rid of me
I am strong
I'm a warrior
Those lies they tell me
I'm so tired and done
You will not become number one
I was shut down
I was so done
They try to bring me down
But I know where I came from

We are leaders
We are warriors
Words can't defeat me

So show me who you are meant to be

Written by: Nya Roper

BRIDGET ROBINSON

As water reflects the face,
so one's life reflects the heart.
Proverbs 27:19

About the Author

Bridget Robinson, a woman of God, a poet, open mic performer, an author, a Kids Ministry Leader and teacher, full-time professional in the legal industry, and profound mother and friend. She is known for her caring heart, warm and bubbly spirit. Born and raised in Tyler, Texas, currently resides in Forney, Texas with her three children: Tay, Nyle and Nya Roper.

Bridget started back writing inspirational poetry after the loss of her father in 2011. Her passion to write and perform continues to grow. She desires her poems to touch every heart across this world as she continues to inspire with her words and share it with everyone.

Made in the USA
Coppell, TX
19 January 2020